BYRON SCOTT

MIKE BIBBY

JASON WILLIAMS

SHAREEF ABDUR-RAHIM

GEORGE LYNCH

BRYANT REEVES

ANTHONY PEELER

GREG ANTHONY

MICHAEL DICKERSON

SHANE BATTIER

BLUE EDWARDS

STROMILE SWIFT

CREATIVE EDUCATION
MICHAEL E. GOODMAN

Published by Creative Education, 123 South Broad Street, Mankato, MN 56001

Creative Education is an imprint of The Creative Company.

Designed by Rita Marshall

Photos by Rich Kane, NBA Photos, SportsChrome

Library of Congress Cataloging-in-Publication Data

Goodman, Michael E. The history of the Memphis Grizzlies / by Michael E. Goodman.

p. cm. — (Pro basketball today)   ISBN 1-58341-117-8

1. Memphis Grizzlies (Basketball team)—History—

Juvenile literature. [1. Memphis Grizzlies (Basketball team)—History.

2. Basketball—History.] I. Title. II. Series.

GV885.52.V36 G65 2001   796.323'64'0971133—dc21   00-047334

First Edition 9 8 7 6 5 4 3 2 1

J
796.323
B00

AROUND 3500 B.C.,

THE ANCIENT EGYPTIANS ESTABLISHED

THEIR CAPITAL CITY ALONG THE BANKS OF THE NILE RIVER

and named it Memphis. More than 5,000 years later, in 1819, United

States General and future president Andrew Jackson founded a new

settlement along the banks of the Mississippi River in Tennessee and

called it Memphis.

During its first 150 years, Memphis, Tennessee, became famous as a

key site for the export of cotton and the development of blues music.

In recent years, the city has drawn millions of tourists eager to see such

local attractions as Graceland, the home of legendary singer Elvis

CHRIS KING

Presley. In 2001, a new attraction arrived in Memphis. That summer, a National Basketball Association (NBA) franchise called the Grizzlies

Before being accepted into the NBA, the prospective Vancouver team was called the "Mounties."

relocated from Canada and began a new life in Tennessee.

{FOUNDING THE FRANCHISE} The Grizzlies started out nearly 2,000 miles from Memphis in Vancouver, British Columbia. Founded in 1995, the Vancouver Grizzlies franchise was the brainchild of local business-

man Arthur Griffiths, whose optimism and determination helped him defy the odds and establish an NBA team in western Canada.

Griffiths knew that sports fans in the area were more interested in hockey than basketball. After all, his family was the longtime owner of the Vancouver Canucks, a team in the National Hockey League. Yet he strongly believed that basketball could also find a place in the hearts of Canadian fans and that Vancouver was the right place for a new NBA

STROMILE SWIFT

Stu Jackson
arrived after
a stint as the
head coach
at the
University of
Wisconsin.

STU JACKSON

franchise. Griffiths's optimism and dedication won over NBA officials, who, in February 1994, approved the addition of a Vancouver franchise to the league. Two days later, the club began selling season tickets and received deposits from 1,100 enthusiastic fans on the first day.

It was a great start, but the new team still needed a general manager, a coach, and players. All of them would have to be in place by the fall of 1995—just 18 months away. Griffiths started at the top and began asking basketball experts who would be the best choice to oversee the building of a new NBA franchise. One name was near the top of everyone's list: Stu Jackson. Jackson had coached successfully in the NBA and college, and he had roots in the Pacific Northwest, having played college ball at the University of Oregon. Griffiths met with Jackson in July 1994, and the two hit it off

Before joining the Grizzlies, guard Lawrence Moten became Syracuse's all-time leading scorer.

LAWRENCE MOTEN

At 6-foot-9 and 240 pounds, Shareef Abdur-Rahim was both fast and powerful.

SHAREEF ABDUR-RAHIM

immediately. Jackson soon came on board as the Grizzlies' first president and general manager.

One of Jackson's first moves was to hire a head coach. He found the man he wanted on the other side of North America: Atlanta Hawks assistant coach Brian Winters. Winters had spent 18 years in the NBA—nine as a player and nine more as an assistant coach. During those years, he had played under or worked with two of the finest coaches in NBA history, Don Nelson and Lenny Wilkens. Now he was ready to put that experience to use.

Winters was hired on June 19, 1995, and immediately set to work. Both the expansion and college drafts were only days away, and Jackson and Winters had to evaluate the talent available for the Grizzlies and put together the club's first roster.

Before his coaching days, Brian Winters was an All-Star guard with the Milwaukee Bucks.

12

GREG ANTHONY

{**GREG, BYRON, AND BLUE**} The Vancouver brain trust

selected 13 players in the expansion draft of veterans from other NBA

teams, hoping that some of them would help the Grizzlies get off to a

successful start. The most important acquisitions were point guard Greg

Anthony from the New York Knicks, veteran shooting guard Byron

Scott from the Indiana Pacers, and speedy swingman Theodore "Blue"

Edwards from the Utah Jazz. All three players brought experience as winners to Vancouver.

The Grizzlies used one of their expansion picks on veteran center Benoit Benjamin.

The Grizzlies made Anthony their first pick because of his leadership qualities and ball-handling skills. He had been the floor general of the 1990 NCAA champion University of Nevada-Las Vegas Runnin' Rebels. After being drafted in the first round by the Knicks in 1991, he developed into a solid backup point guard for a strong New York team.

While Anthony had been drafted to direct the Grizzlies' offensive attack, Scott and Edwards were chosen for their scoring ability. Scott had earned three championship rings playing alongside Magic Johnson with the Los Angeles Lakers in the 1980s. During his 12 NBA seasons, he had tallied nearly 14,000 points, and he planned to add to that total in Vancouver. Edwards's main weapons were his blinding speed, terrific

BYRON SCOTT

leaping ability, and reckless determination on the court. The Grizzlies

knew they would need all of those talents and more if they were going

to succeed in their first campaign.

{IT'S A BIG COUNTRY} The club still needed a "man in the

middle," a bruising center who could score, rebound, and be a defensive

force under the basket. Vancouver recognized that it would help if that player could also have real fan appeal. The Grizzlies got all of those

qualities in their first-ever NBA Draft pick, Bryant "Big Country" Reeves

from Oklahoma State.

Reeves was a young giant whose nickname fit him

perfectly. At 7-feet and 295 pounds, he was obviously big.

And having been brought up on a farm in tiny Gans,

Oklahoma (251 people and no stop lights), he was defi-

nitely a country boy. Reeves had enjoyed a great senior season at

Oklahoma State, leading the Cowboys to the Big Eight championship and

to a Final Four berth in the 1995 NCAA tournament. His strong inside

game and willingness to learn had earned praise from coaches and scouts

around the country. "I've always liked his game," commented Bill Walton,

a former All-Star center and television analyst. "He's learned the physical

part of the game. All the raw material, all the potential, is there."

Rookie Bryant Reeves proved his worth with 13 points and 7 rebounds a game.

BRYANT REEVES

Guard Damon Jones was one of several talented ball handlers in the team's short history.

Fans in western Canada immediately fell in love with Reeves's

country charm and unspoiled attitude. The Grizzlies sponsored a spe-

cial "Hair Country" promotion midway through the

1995–96 season. Any fans who were willing to have their

hair shaved in a flattop buzz cut like Big Country's would

get free tickets to that night's game. More than 2,000

Vancouver fans, including 18 women, lined up before the

game to become Big Country look-alikes.

Coach Winters got the new Grizzlies off to a great start as the

club won the first two games in its history. Then reality set in as the

team experienced some growing pains. The Grizzlies lost their next 19

games before finally defeating the Portland Trail Blazers in overtime in

their 22nd game. Later in the season, injuries began to hurt the team,

and Vancouver fell into another downward spiral. This time, the club

ERIC MURDOCH

lost 23 games in a row, setting a dubious new NBA record.

Still, many of the losses were close contests, and Vancouver fans,

who packed General Motors Place for nearly all of the team's home

games, took pride in how hard their undermanned Grizzlies played.

After the season, Stu Jackson set out to reward the fans' faith in the

new team by improving it.

{SHAREEF SOARS IN} The Grizzlies' first step was to strength-

en their front line by getting some help for Reeves. "For Bryant to be

A fearsome defender, forward Roy Rogers rejected two shots a game in **1996–97**.

effective, it's absolutely essential that we have quick play-

ers on either side of him to open up the middle and help

with the rebounding and scoring," explained assistant

coach Rex Hughes. With that in mind, the Grizzlies made

some key moves before the 1996 NBA Draft, trading for

power forward Pete Chilcutt and small forward George Lynch. They

also signed sharpshooting guard Anthony Peeler to provide instant

offense from the outside.

Then, picking third overall in the NBA Draft, Vancouver selected

19-year-old forward Shareef Abdur-Rahim, who had decided to turn pro

after only one year at the University of California. In his only college

season, Abdur-Rahim had led the Cal Golden Bears in scoring, rebound-

ROY ROGERS

Anthony Peeler was one of the NBA's deadliest marksmen from the perimeter.

ANTHONY PEELER

ing, and steals and had become the first freshman ever named Pac 10 Conference Player of the Year. Now he was ready to make the transition from Bear to Grizzly.

The day Abdur-Rahim arrived at training camp before the 1996–97 season, Blue Edwards decided to put the rookie to the test. Edwards guarded the youngster and made him look bad on several plays. Then it was the

Veteran Blue Edwards led the young Grizzlies with his physical style of play.

rookie's turn. On one memorable play, Abdur-Rahim squared up to Edwards, faked left, and then slashed right. Near the foul line, he went airborne, sailing past Edwards and stuffing the ball with authority. Even the veterans had to cheer. It was clear that the team's new leader had arrived, and fans soon gave him a special nickname—"the Future."

Abdur-Rahim quickly became a star on and off the court. In his first year in Vancouver, he averaged 18 points and almost 7 rebounds

BLUE EDWARDS

per game, good enough to earn a place on the NBA All-Rookie first

team. He improved on those numbers in his second and third years,

ranking sixth and then fourth in the league in scoring. His superstar

status was made official when he was chosen as a member of the U.S.

basketball team that captured the gold medal at the 2000 Summer

Olympics in Sydney, Australia.

{THE WILDCAT CONNECTION} An improved frontcourt, led by Abdur-Rahim and Big Country Reeves, helped the Grizzlies become more competitive. Yet the team still lost too many close contests, and a series of coaches came and went.

The good news for Grizzlies fans was that several talented new players also began arriving in Vancouver via trades and the NBA Draft. The Grizzlies used their first pick in the 1998 Draft to take point guard Mike Bibby, an All-American who had led the Arizona Wildcats to the NCAA championship just months earlier. Bibby, whose father Henry was also an NBA point guard in the '70s, was a great ball handler who cared more about giving his teammates scoring opportunities than padding his own statistics.

During his second season with the Grizzlies, Bibby was joined in Vancouver by his former Arizona teammate Michael Dickerson.

Vancouver added a strong rebounder by trading for Michael Smith in **1997–98**.

MICHAEL SMITH

Dickerson arrived via a blockbuster trade with the Houston Rockets for

the Grizzlies' top pick in the 1999 NBA Draft, guard Steve Francis. The

"Wildcat Connection" gave the Grizzlies one of the top

young backcourt duos in the league. Together, Bibby and

Dickerson averaged 32 points, 7 rebounds, and nearly 11

assists per game in 1999–00.

Three other key pieces were added before the

2000–01 season. First, the Grizzlies improved their roster by trading for

backup center Ike Austin and selecting forward Stromile Swift from

Louisiana State University with the second overall pick in the 2000

NBA Draft. New Vancouver general manager Billy Knight (who replaced

Jackson midway through the 1999–00 season) described the athletic

6-foot-9 "Stro" as "a young colt ready to stand in the winner's circle."

The third key addition was new head coach Sidney Lowe. From his

OTHELLA HARRINGTON

college days as point guard on the 1983 "miracle" NCAA champion North Carolina State Wolfpack team to his years in the NBA as a player and coach, Lowe had learned that the secrets to winning are defense and teamwork. Upon his arrival, Lowe made it clear that he expected hard work from his players and assured fans that the hard work would produce winning results.

Veteran forward Grant Long was a key rebounder off the bench in **1999–00** and **2000–01**.

Despite the changes, the club continued to struggle in 2000–01. As the team stumbled to a 23–59 finish, its fan support dwindled. After the season, a major shakeup was set into motion during the 2001 NBA Draft. In one amazing day, Shareef Abdur-Rahim was traded to Atlanta for the draft rights to Spanish center Pau Gasol; the club drafted Duke University forward Shane Battier, the College Player of the Year; and Mike Bibby was sent to Sacramento in exchange for one of the league's

GRANT LONG

Michael
Dickerson
added speed
and scoring
potential to
the Grizzlies'
lineup.

MICHAEL DICKERSON

Known as an outstanding ball handler, Mike Bibby led Vancouver for three seasons.

MIKE BIBBY

flashiest point guards, Jason Williams.

But the biggest change was still to come. Less than a week after the draft, the NBA's Board of Governors approved the sale of the Grizzlies to a group of businessmen in Memphis and the relocation of the club from Canada to Tennessee. "We're obviously looking forward to the start of the season and the start of a lifetime here," said Billy Knight. "It's time for this [team] to go in a different direction."

32

The Grizzlies franchise suffered through serious growing pains during its early years in the NBA, but with a new home and a new attitude, the team is eager to claw its way up the standings in Tennessee. With an exciting mix of young stars and solid veterans on their roster, the new Memphis Grizzlies hope to stand in the winner's circle often in the seasons ahead.

Hardworking forward Shane Battier gave the Grizzlies hope for a successful start in Memphis.

SHANE BATTIER